WHITE CLOUDS
BLUE RAIN

T0363208

By the same author:

I don't know how that happened (2020)

WHITE CLOUDS
BLUE RAIN

OLIVER DRISCOLL

RECENT
WORK
PRESS

White Clouds Blue Rain
Recent Work Press
Canberra, Australia

Copyright © Oliver Driscoll, 2021

ISBN: 9780645009088 (paperback)

 A catalogue record for this
work is available from the
National Library of Australia

Cover image: 'Chair with woodworm' © Matt Leaves, 2016. Reproduced with permission.
Cover design: Recent Work Press
Set by Recent Work Press

recentworkpress.com

SS

For Amelia, Una and Matai

What's best is simply to look at people.

—Alberto Giacometti

Out of nowhere
I recalled a video taken by a friend's father
of a tugboat churning through water

Great chains ran from its back
but whatever it was that was being towed
remained out of view

The figures on board were moving quickly

I cannot recall there having been sound
with the footage
or whether it was in colour

Now, I am confronted with the squeak of rubber
boots on metal

and the repetition of the still hard seawater
against the rounded hull

I dreamt last night my mother had died. In her room, in our old house in the north-east of this country, long ago sold, I was going through her things. My sister and one of my brothers were with me. Early morning light came through orange and green glass louvres. Outside, below the louvres, I knew there to be a narrow sleeper staircase running down the bank to the underside of the house and, behind another wall, a garden bed densely planted with bird of paradise.

Across from the bed, behind a calico curtain, there was a shelf of Penguin novels with orange and pale-green spines. I removed a book called *Deborah's Square* from the shelf. The cover had an inset border of thin royal blue and turquoise lines around a sepia-toned drawing of a woman sitting on a chair pulled away from a table. There were several books on the shelf in the same series, all with identical borders and images but different titles.

I would take one of the books from the shelf, turn it over, read the back, and then pass it to my sister, who would do the same before passing it to my brother.

After placing my hand within the gap I'd made on the shelf, I left the room, suddenly distraught, and walked through the living room, and then out through the French doors onto the balcony and sat at the top of the staircase. In front of me there was a great big cypress that never, in life, existed.

In bed this morning, I recalled watching my father hack the staircase into the bank with a mattock and a shovel. The louvres had not in life been glass but white painted timber. I thought to myself that the dream had felt like silt.

There seemed to be something incredibly sad, I thought, about the whiteness of the house, the way the sun would light up its big triangular face. I had a strong sense that I should phone my mother to make sure she was okay.

Two years ago, I planted small eucalypts along our apartment block's driveway, where it passes our bedroom. Yesterday afternoon, through our bedroom window, I saw that a neighbour who plays the double bass was pulling the trees tight up against the fence with black zip ties. A bag of the ties was lying on the asphalt by his feet. I went out to the driveway and said I don't think we should do that. Why not, he replied, because they're plastic? He pulled another of the trees hard up against the fence and I left him there.

In the early evening the weather turned. Through the window I watched the trees thrash around in the wind.

Worried that the trees would be badly damaged, I put on a raincoat and went back out to the driveway and cut the zip ties away. I then pulled and tied each of the trees against the fence with heavy twine. I held the spool of twine beneath my arm to keep it out of the rain.

It wasn't yet dark but a circular light above an entrance on the building next door, on the other side of the fence, was already on. One end of a blue tarpaulin had become detached from a trailer parked beside the entrance. The tarpaulin was buckling into triangles and dome-like arcs. I was filled with a sense of comfort and shelter and familiarity.

Back inside, I read an interview with a German author who had moved to the UK in his early twenties. He'd found himself at home there, he said, because of the dampened light and the reserve. I tried, as I often do, to imagine never having returned from there myself, to recreate the qualities of the light and space I'd experienced there. I'd noticed recently that while I continue to long for elsewhere, particularly places I've lived previously, as frequently as ever, the feeling has become less overwhelming, and is now almost a sensation I can escape to rather than one I need to escape from.

Reading the interview, I wondered what, if anything, would be left in its place if the intensity of longing for alternative lives was to reduce almost to nothing.

After getting out of bed this morning I checked on the eucalypts. They had been chaffed by the ties, but not severely. There would likely always be a line around the trunks, I thought, and the lines may, in time, become more visible, but they wouldn't be of any real concern. On the way back through the car park to our apartment, I noticed small white sachets with 'salt' written on them in pale blue letters in one of the parking spaces, next to an oil stain. They were wet from last night's rain and tore in my hands when I picked them up. I scrunched them together, the salt grinding away the sodden paper.

The soil here is almost entirely sand. At the base of a downpipe at the back corner of the building, near the eucalypts, the sand has washed clean.

Back inside, I made tea and toast and brought them through to the dining table in the living room. I had a text from my mother that read, Correction from my idiot phone: darker, bunny, know. I scrolled up. Her previous text was three days earlier.

As I washed the dishes and boiled the kettle again to refill the teapot, I saw two of my neighbours talking in the car park. My German neighbour pointed up towards her apartment, and then the other neighbour, Kelly, pointed down the driveway towards hers.

Later, I went out walking. A number of branches in the area had been brought down in the storm. Two streets over, a tree had sheared off just metres from the ground, leaving a thick spike. The tree had fallen away from the house behind, and through the front fence. It seemed miraculous that it would break apart so near to the base.

This morning, I cut back the ivy on the tall fence that runs along half of our block's rear boundary. When we first moved in, the ivy had spread across onto the roof of the garages that run the width of the block just in front of the fence. Early on, I'd cut my way into the cavity beneath with gardening shears. There had been a domed ivy thatch of roof over the darkened interior. The ground had clicked and moved. When I'd scuffed the leaf litter with my shoes, I'd seen that I'd been standing on broken-up roof tiles. I'd realised suddenly it wasn't silent, that the ivy overhead had hummed with bees.

A short while later, tree loppers had cut away the ivy, after which I'd pulled out the roof tiles and the rest of the rubbish that had accumulated back there. Along with much else, there had been a small plastic Christmas tree; a red dog or cat collar with a leather tag with 'Jupiter' debossed into it; a car battery; old hooks and brackets; a candle snuffer; hundreds of small bottles, some broken, some intact, that appeared to have been used by an artist; the torso of a Ken doll and one of his shoes; marbles; coins; a bank card; an unbroken square of glass the size of a passport; a camera case; and a Walkman filled with earth. The headphone cable was still plugged into the Walkman but had been cut a few inches along. As I dug the objects out, I thought perhaps I should stop what I was doing, that one day if we were to have a child, I could dig here with them, as a treasure hunt. This child would have loved, I thought, the feeling of the now cut-away inverted hull of ivy overhead.

This morning, after I cut away the lower branches, I retrieved my ladder from my studio to cut higher. As I cut, fine wet powder fell into my eyes. The ground was soft and uneven from the digging and from the leaves and branches I'd thrown down there. It was difficult to make the ladder stable. Amongst the rotting boards of the fence, tucked up against a post, I found an old bird's nest.

Five or six years ago, my paternal grandfather said to me that his own father had been at the top of a ladder painting a terrace in midwinter when someone had stolen his coat and wallet that he'd left below. He'd then had to walk home in the rain. This was in the north of London, my grandfather had said, not far from where he himself had lived for much of his life. His father had, he'd continued, soon died of pneumonia. At the time, my partner and I, along with my father and grandfather, were staying with my aunt and uncle in their house on the outskirts of Colchester over Christmas.

On the Christmas evening, after eating and drinking and playing board games, we'd put on wellingtons and heavy raincoats and walked across paddocks, each with our own torch. My grandfather had remained behind by the heater with a blanket tucked firmly around him. As we'd made our way across the sodden fields, I told my father about the conversation. He said he'd never heard the story before, he'd only known that his father's father had died when his father had been a child. Never having known him, he went on, I've never really thought of him as my grandfather, but I suppose that's exactly what he was to me. My poor dad, he said, pulling ahead of my partner and me to catch up with his sister and her husband.

We came to a small round lake, the water black in the dark. A dinghy was lit up towards the middle. Two figures could be made out, an adult and a child, sitting at either end of the dinghy, holding fishing rods. My uncle said, who's swimming, and stripped down to a pair of knee-length swimmers. He waded out through the reeds and dived. My partner lent against me, sliding her arms into my jacket. My father took off his shoes and rolled up his trousers and waded in a short way. My uncle turned to us and I directed my torch onto him. He then turned again and swam towards the boat, disappearing in the dark. When he reappeared in the light of the boat, my aunty said, they're friends of ours. He stopped swimming and I could hear that he and the two on the water were talking. Golly it's cold, my father said, stepping out from the reeds.

Before we'd left on the walk, my grandfather had become mad. We'd finished up the board games and were chatting, sitting on the sofa and lounge chairs. Suddenly he'd said, when are you going to let me sing. You can sing if you want to, my father had said, is there a song we should put on for you. I want to sing, I want to sing, he'd said, unsoothed.

When I was finished cutting the ivy back to the fence, I cut the branches on the ground into smaller sections, so that they would form less of a tangled nest. When I came back to the car park my neighbour who plays the double bass was in his garage. He had doors from his apartment up on saw horses. He said, I'm sorry if I was rough with the trees, but they did need to be tied back. I said that's okay, and yes, they did. He said he'd had to go twice today to a suburb further around the bay because they'd made his doors the wrong thickness. Look he said, gesturing for me to compare one of the original unpainted timber doors to a white MDF reproduction.

Last night in bed I was reading a Japanese novel from the beginning of the twentieth century. In the novel, a man says to a woman sitting across from him on the train, who he's only just met, that he's unable to read Western novels from beginning to end, that the only way he's able to read them is by reading a passage here, a passage there. A moment later he says, we don't know what we're getting into by cramming ourselves into train carriages like this.

A couple of weeks ago, my mother sent me photos of the inside of her kiln. By text she wrote that my sister's two-year-old had thrown the nicest pot down her front stairs. Some pots, she wrote, have a lifefulness, but most do not. This one did, she wrote. She'd had to remove everything from the bottom two shelves of the cabinet in the living room. I don't remember you children being like that, she continued, he grabs at things constantly.

A few nights ago, my partner and I went to a friend's new apartment. Over dinner, a woman we hadn't previously met spoke about the simple timber house or cabin really on the coast that her family had lived in until she was twelve or thirteen. The openings, she said, had all been louvres and slats and sometimes, even during the coldest months, she and her brothers would sleep on the open balcony. At times, she said, we'd wake up being lashed with rain. She said she always had trouble articulating this, but that she can't help but feel that memory is deeply connected to our experience of weather. Now, she continued, living in an apartment not dissimilar to the one we were in, a little smaller, perhaps, and a little higher from the ground, but essentially the same, the memories she was forming seemed insubstantial, somehow slight or weightless. I don't think they'll stay, or if they do, that they'll be moving in their recollection. When it's raining heavily or just cold and damp, she has the sensation that memory is located on the other side of her apartment walls.

While out walking this afternoon, I was caught in a cold brief rain shower. I walked a short way down a driveway and stood under a balcony over the car park gate. The wall next to me was layered in glazed red and rough black metallic bricks. A clear plastic basketball backboard was lying on the gravel at the base of the wall with a plastic bag full of lemons sitting where there would normally be a hoop. Two women were in a car parked on the street, likely also waiting for a break in the rain. On a podcast I was listening to a woman said, Christianity, with its turn away from animism and with an un-earth-bound eternal spirit, provided an escape from the brutality of the natural world. Now, she continued, we want more than anything an escape from the brutality we ourselves inflict on the natural world.

When the rain eased, the two women rushed out of the car and disappeared from view. I continued on, and a few streets away, I heard what sounded like large sheets of velcro being slowly pulled apart. It was, I realised a moment later, rain falling from a tree's canopy onto a trampoline. Pink flowers had been walked into the wet asphalt footpath. Further along, on the corner, I'd often seen a man in his sixties or seventies, frequently shirtless, slowly stripping back a split-level townhouse. He'd removed the awnings, the decking boards from a small Juliette balcony, and taken out the windows, which he'd covered over with milky plastic sheeting, stuck to the walls with blue duct tape. His tiny front yard was still full of metal and timber. I hadn't, however, seen him for months.

On the way back, I walked down the street with the tree that had come down in the storm. The tree had been cut into blocks that, along with foliage and pieces of broken fence, were still spread across the pavement and the verge. Two men were carrying the blocks and black plastic tubs full of leaves and branches across the road to a trailer.

When I drove down the street later this evening, I saw that much of the tree and fence were still there.

In a passage I read in bed last night from the Japanese novel, the man says he's never been able to comprehend other people because he's never felt hunger, which, he's come to understand, observing but not experiencing it, impinges heavily on everything that is done.

Yesterday morning while having breakfast, I watched from the dining table in the living room as a man in white overalls from the company that is soon to repair and paint the building's windows moved a ladder from tree to tree along our driveway marking branches with white paint that will have to be removed to allow the cherry picker access. There was a knock on the door. I opened it holding my mug of tea. Kelly had come to ask me if I would feed her cat while she was away next week. Sorry for the late notice, she said, I forget about the poor little honey.

Later when I went out, I noticed that the man had left white paint marks on two branches of a wattle with weathered and craggy bark in the centre of the front garden. The branches of the tree sweep down and then up. One of the larger branches came down in a storm several months ago. Now, it'll have none left on that side, the side facing the building.

When I answered her phone call this morning, my mother said, terrible news, our house has sold again. She'd been having dreams all year where she was back inside the house, along with King and Christmas, only, in one of the dreams, King was the mother cat, and Christmas the son. I chuckled at idea of big dopey King being the mother. I've thought about this since the dream, she said seriously, and I think he would have been a very good mother.

On the phone, I said that I too had recently dreamt about our house, though I didn't tell her that, in the dream, she had recently passed away. I'm glad you dream about the house too, she said, I'm sure my other children don't. They won't hear about it, she said.

At the supermarket today, a man at the self-service register next to mine was attempting to peel the barcode away from the cellophane around a bouquet of flowers. A woman on his far side smiled at him.

My partner left a perfect coil of orange peel on a timber cutting board on the kitchen bench when she left this morning before I woke. I picked the coil up by one end and let it spring up and down. I went out into the courtyard. The sky was clear but the asphalt wet as though it had just rained. Later when I went out again, the sky was heavily overcast but the asphalt dry.

My partner and I went up to Kelly's apartment last night to be given her keys and to be introduced to her cat and shown how to feed her. When we arrived, the cat was a lump under the blankets in the centre of Kelly's bed. Kelly pulled the cat out and put her on a rug that runs down the centre of the hallway. Surprisingly, the cat remained where she had been placed. We chatted in the hallway and after a while I knelt down next to the cat. She twisted her torso around so that her belly faced upward. When I moved to pat her, she hissed at me.

After we left, my partner asked if I recalled the white cat from Lisbon. Night after night, the white cat would yowl on the cobblestones below our window and then, each night, would roll over in front of the same male cat. But then when he neared, she would stand and hiss and fight him off, the two of them shrieking.

Learning to live with the
willed lack of silence
of everyday objects
A piece of smoothened
amber glass that looks
like the nose
of a subsiding face and
that feels stone-like
That whatever can be
done has to be done
knowing that nothing is
constant or stable, neither
the thing itself, nor our experience
of it. In the car park, I unfold
a big, blue muddy tarpaulin
and hose it down, the water
running to a drain under
a neighbour's white car.

On the Friday just past, my partner and I drove north to the alpine region. Halfway there we stopped at a small park with a dry but overgrown creek bed on one side and a tall barbed wire fence on another. By the road, there were three life-sized bronze statues of men who'd left the town to fight in the First World War and had been killed. Two of the men had died in their early twenties, the third in his mid-fifties. The statues must have been modelled, I thought, from photographs.

There was a heavy artillery gun further into the park, by the creek, well away from the figures. We sat at a table near the gun and ate cucumber and cheese sandwiches, and I recalled the intense romance I'd felt as a young child towards the men I'd seen in a film or in photographs wearing rolled-up khaki shorts, leather boots and white t-shirts on a flat colourless plane firing artillery guns like this one. The feeling, I thought, had been closely associated with the men's clothing and how it had been worn.

Tom and Anne, a couple in their eighties, greeted us at the end of the driveway when we arrived at their bed and breakfast some hours later. They both wore wide-brimmed hats and removed gardening gloves as they walked over to our car. We were staying in a cabin attached to the back of their small house towards the centre of a large carefully composed garden.

After we brought our bags up from the car, my partner went for a walk around the garden while I sat on the balcony observing the birds and reading a novel written in the late forties. A couple on the precipice of falling out of love are, in the book, travelling around North Africa with a kind of recklessness and aimlessness immediately after the end of the Second World War. Any travel infrastructure that had existed prior to the war is gone. The woman can no longer stand to be intimate with her husband.

In the garden, a sprinkler had been placed on a browned-off patch of grass by a copse of silver birches. My partner appeared from behind a hedge. When I looked up again a moment later, she was once more out of view.

Several years ago, while we were standing in the carpeted hallway outside her office, my then secondary thesis supervisor had said she'd been reading the same novel and asked if I ever had. I said I'd started reading it a number of times but had never made it far into the work. She said this is precisely how it had been with her. But, she said, it was because she had been too young. Now, she went on, shaking her head, she no longer was. What could I now be said to be too young for, she said, laughing, the last things were crossed off many years ago. Death, I proposed, trying to be kind. No one, she said, is ever too young for that. I have passed through, she said, the penultimate membrane and only have that last one to encounter.

My secondary supervisor then said that the novel has, in her mind, two central concerns, that of dying, that which none of us are too young for, as well as what we're willing to do to ourselves and others when we are not dying. It's about, she said, how men live with shame and women with anger, and how both shame and anger end in the abasement of oneself or of another. It will be there, she said. I asked if she was referring to literature or to life. Ha, she said, I look forward to our next meeting. She put her hand briefly on my shoulder before going back into her office and closing her door.

This time, the novel had clicked, and I was inside its angular brilliance. It caught something of, I thought, the impossibility we have of untethering ourselves from others, from ideas we have about ourselves, and from memory, and the reverse impossibility of absolute nearness and inter-reliance. There is no ideal form of relationship, I thought while reading the book, one can have with memory.

When my partner returned, she said she'd come across a deep-green lagoon in the far corner of the property, bordered on two sides by a blue electric fence. She pointed in the direction of the lagoon. I must have seen her, I thought, just before she'd come across it. She said two geese had been sitting on one side of the lagoon under a tree, and two ducks on the other side, under another tree.

Late that evening, after we swam in a nearby dam and walked up to a series of weathered settler huts, I received a phone call from a friend of ours who was staying in our apartment looking after our cat while we were away. Seeing his name appear, I was worried. He said, I'm sorry, I'm such a moron, but I can't light your oven. The door, I explained, had to be all the way open when you pressed the ignition, or nothing would happen. He said, there, I see the flame. I'm such a moron, he said again. Please don't worry, I said, it had taken us months to work this out. I reminded him that he needed to let the vanity tap run hot before turning on the shower, otherwise the hot water would disappear altogether. The moron remembers that one, he said.

When I'd called this friend a week earlier to ask him to stay, I'd mentioned that I'd recently read an essay by the author he was writing a short monograph on. I admired the author greatly, but said this essay had frustrated me. She had been so gleeful, I said, about how badly she'd treated people who had themselves treated her poorly, or whom she'd perceived to have done so. I said an essay can't do everything, but this one doesn't lead to any kind of understanding, only to resolve. She seems, I said, to enjoy wilfully misinterpreting the actions of others.

One of the people the author had described scolding was a young man working in a bar whose behaviour, I thought, was largely bound by the nature of his service job. She was looking down at him, and his silly job. She detailed the orders she'd given to the young man, and his reaction to each. My friend said to me, the difference between himself and the author was that she had absolute faith in the idea that it was inherently valuable to get her full self onto the page. Our true self, he went on, is frequently irrationally angry.

On the drive up to the alpine region, my partner and I had discussed the author at length. There is so much power, my partner had said, in anger, and many people, including herself, can't help but conform to the strong judgement of others, even when that judgement is evidently unjustified or even cruel. On the page, she'd continued, it's hard to honestly condemn yourself, your anger, without simultaneously furnishing it with a moral core, especially over the course of a career. What is that anger, she'd said, the second or third time it's represented. Besides, she'd gone on, if we remain bound to narrative and to the dramatic arc, anger from life will always be transformed and amplified on the page. It will be made meaningful, she'd said.

In the crisp early morning light the following day, as my partner slept, I again sat on the balcony and read the novel. Four king parrot tails hung down from the roof sheeting, flicking back and forth. When I next looked up from the page, the birds swooped quickly down together into the foliage of a Japanese maple.

I could see Anne down at the far end of the garden on her knees, her back to me, wearing red slacks, her torso within the foliage of a silvery garden bed. She couldn't possibly experience the beauty of the property, I thought, in the half-seen uncomplicated way that her visitors would. Instead, I thought, she would see only tasks that needed doing, and the accumulated effort of those already done. Perhaps, I thought, the only way for her to experience the beauty of the garden was through her guests.

The husband in the novel is gradually overcome with fever. He's pitifully cold. He and his wife travel by bus and then by truck southward, towards a town deeper in the desert where he will, they hope, finally be warm. By the time they arrive in the town, however, he's drifting in and out of consciousness and seems to be on the cusp of passing away. The woman says to herself, this is the test, this is where she will require the resolve to think clearly and make decisions correctly. It can only remain unclear to her, however, whether she has arrived at the time to devote herself to their fractured relationship or to finally disentangle herself.

On our drive back from the region, we stopped at a lookout next to three identical Honda motorcycles that had earlier raced by us on the winding road. In the distance, there was a ring of mountains. On the plain below, a boat slowly moved diagonally across what appeared to be an artificial lake, the unwavering triangle of wake seemingly out of scale with the body of water and the tiny boat it was trailing.

In khaki
at seven
a war child
thumbnail running along a thread of cotton
hours alone on the ground
by a white timber post
crushing ants that are green and amber
how loudly can you scream
let me see it let me have it
spans of time and makes of cars
the deepest hole you can dig
blisters and the shovel's blade
cutting through earth that's always been there
leaving a mound and then a basin
moods, sensations wait around
holding an electric sander
the hillside has been cleared and cut
fluorescent pink and green on shiny black
to see parallel bars flex and spring
you could have killed yourselves and me
2E, 3M
falling on grass
changing schools

Yesterday, I listened to a recording of a poet reading a long poem. In the poem, he describes seeing a potter in India sitting on the ground, spinning the wheel with one hand to throw the small cups that were used, after a bisque firing, at the adjacent tea stand. After they were used, the cups were dropped onto the ground, returning to the mud, the poet said. My mother had told me about using rough unglazed cups while on a train going through India. After using them, she said, you threw them out the window. The poet had, however, kept his cup and it now sat before him on his desk. He couldn't help, he said, but feel a greater remorse for this small break in this cycle than he did about many things, such as his betrayal of loved ones.

This morning, on the phone, my mother told me that my sister had, before leaving, painted the fibre cement walls of her shower. When my mother had said to her, you can't do that, this is a rental, my sister had replied, but you let him, as in me, paint the floor. My sister had then said, he's your favourite though, isn't he. I said I'd painted the floor because it was peeling back to what looked like a red-lead undercoat. I was worried about my sister's child. I didn't paint it for fun, I said, I would have preferred not to have painted that floor. Yes, my mother replied, because it might have been poison.

While talking on the phone, she said she was walking back from her pottery studio with the bub strolling slowly but confidently beside her. It was too hard, she said, to push the stroller along the dirt road. She lives in a small yellow timber worker's cottage on the site of what was once a timber mill. Her studio is in one of the mill buildings, adjacent to the workspace of two young men who make heavy furniture out of rainforest timbers. The rest of the mill buildings are either empty or are used as storage.

Her cottage is one of four in a row and is divided by two intersecting walls into four small rooms of equal size, with a lean-to bathroom off from one side on a concrete slab. When she first described the cottage to me, I said, it sounds just like Van Gogh and Gauguin's Yellow House in Arles. Yes, she said, she knows. Perhaps, she said, there's something unhealthy about having all of the rooms the same size. Her ceilings are unaccountably high. They must have just had a lot of timber, she said when I'd visited her and had pointed this out.

The last time I'd visited her, while walking back from her studio to her cottage, as she was now doing as we spoke on the phone, we stopped at a small declivity between the mill buildings and the cottages where old machinery, drum barrels, and long thin girders had been dumped and seemed to be slowly sinking into the soil. My mother pointed out a timber and metal caravan-like structure deep in grass. It had been, she said, a food wagon at the top of the range, sixty or eighty years ago, when there had only been the one narrow winding lane. Vehicles, she said, would take turns coming up or going down, and you may have waited for hours.

I stood on what appeared to be an engine partially sunken into the earth beside the wagon. There was a small hook on the side that would have been for an awning cable, I thought. I placed my hand over the hook. It could have come away from the timber panelling with a gentle pull. No, my mother said, please don't. Please just let it rot and rust away together, she said.

As we continued to walk back to her worker's cottage, she said the food wagon had been run by her landlord's grandmother. She's probably still hanging around here, she said, flicking her hands about, we should just leave her in peace.

My mother has had my sister's two-year-old boy now for almost two months. On the phone she told me about how much of a joy he's becoming. She said, he's just like a boy out of an old picture book. There's nothing of his parents, she said. He looks just the way, she went on, my eldest brother, her first child, had looked at that age. When they wake up, she said, they wrestle playfully and then he pulls a big long sad face. She then pulls the same face and he lights up with laughter.

I'm so glad he has you, I said.

A few weeks ago, I placed a plywood sheet over one of the two laundry tubs in my studio as a shelf. I then placed six deep noodle bowls that my mother had thrown while visiting us two or three years ago that I'm still yet to have fired on the shelf.

Last night, I dreamt I knocked the shelf while moving pieces of timber around my studio. In the dream there were small glass and ceramic objects on the shelf, rather than the unfired bowls. Nothing had fallen when the shelf had been knocked, but when I tried to put it back in place, a blown glass tumbler with a blue rim and a green base fell, cracking in two. I awoke relieved that I hadn't, in fact, broken the glass, but then recalled that it had never, in life, existed.

This afternoon, I listened to a recording of a lecture by a painter from the UK. The artist said she mostly paints her three sisters, her mother and her dear friend Angus. If she doesn't know her subject intimately, all she'll be able to do is measure and replicate their appearance precisely, she said. Every once in a while, or every few years really, she continued, she does attempt a self-portrait, though most have been embarrassing. Her son laughed when he saw her most recent one. But she's come to embrace, at least in a small way, the embarrassing nature of the exercise. Even an attempt to be unflattering, she said, is a show of confidence.

Recently, the painter said, she's started to paint multiples of herself together. She'd realised while painting the first of these that, having three siblings, she'd always encountered herself in relation to others with whom she had certain similarities, as part of a set.

I don't know if this still goes on, the painter said later in the lecture, but when I was young, the painters who were men would ask me and everybody else how long each of us painted every day. Needing to be known to paint ten hours a day, she said, was their way of turning everything into elemental survival, to emphasise a clear thing over a less clear thing. But I realised early on, she said, perhaps through their questioning, that I didn't want to or need to paint for very long each day, or even every day. What I mostly do, she continued, is sit down and think. It amuses me a little bit, she said, that, in a sense, what differentiates successful and unsuccessful artworks is the avoidance of what you can't, for whatever reason, do or get away with. It's exhausting, this avoidance, and it takes a great deal of thought and working through, but it's also what makes a great work so pleasing, seeing all the traps the artist hasn't fallen into.

Last night I dreamt that my sister and two men were putting together a compensation claim against a hotel that they'd been brought to by a police officer. My sister had thinned right down. Afterwards, when it was only the two of us left in the room, she said, she'd taken the thing because she could. Crying, I begged her to stop and to look after her child. She then cried herself, not knowing, and perhaps not having any reason to know, that I cared.

This afternoon, when I went to take one of my mother's small celadon beaker-like cups from the cupboard, it slipped from my hand, and trying to catch it, I knocked it across the kitchen. I found it tucked behind the fridge in pieces.

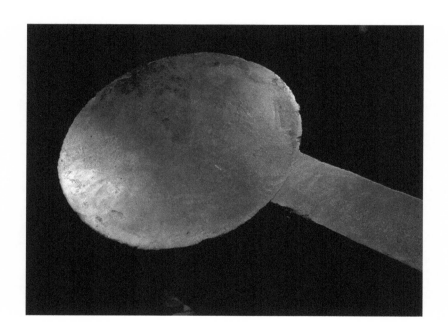

Matchpoint
    Streaks that rest in air

To be had and to home

The lake with pink trees and a dam
Three sides thinning flat and clear

Mussels the size of your thumb

Dried outmossrunningdown one side
Spilling curve of whitened water
Still and dry

Pineapple cut down centre
Face acidic cool
    I'l do it sundae.

If you had to choose between what he knows and what he doesn't
The narrow roads around here

Rough sun
Cold wall
The boy who dropped a glass bottle of water on the floor of the
bakery

A red tennis court crushed into unsold units
With no glass in the windows

A broken cashmere sweater. The

Coldlamboutalone like that

Cat got your back

Three leftover tiles
Stuck into ground

Like a rocket like a steamtrain like a moose buckling at knees

Torch batteries
A lunch fruit

: if in eating unceasingly with the back of a spoon
: if in swimming in darktapping feet ahead of you with each

chop break camel fissure split

Like a sunken record player
Like a new set of bangs

Yellow like gold like stepping onto gravel

Seeing an orchard on a hill
And only then on a plain

Last night was windy and I was woken by what sounded like a soft drink can or a plastic cup being blown up and down our driveway. The can or cup would be quiet for a while and I would think, it's now in a garden bed, it's stopped, but then some minutes later, the small sharp echoes would reappear. Eventually I went out to the driveway, but I couldn't find whatever had been making the sound. Perhaps it had been the trees squeaking against the fence, I thought, but that seemed to be a different sound.

Back in bed, I picked up an essay collection I'd been reading by the Japanese architect Kengo Kuma, opening it to a piece about the Austrian-American architect Rudolph Schindler, whose own house in Hollywood my partner visited several years ago. Schindler had moved from Vienna to Chicago to work for Frank Lloyd Wright and when Wright started to receive commissions on the West Coast, Schindler relocated to LA. Wright himself at that time was travelling back and forth to Tokyo to work on the Imperial Hotel.

Both Wright and Schindler were interested in preformed concrete. Wright's approach was to use the fluidity of the material to ornament his buildings with neo-Mayan reliefs. Schindler on the other hand used preformed concrete to create what Kuma refers to as a democratic architecture—one that was seemingly simple, non-elite and demystified. For his own house, the house that my partner visited, finished in 1922, he pre-poured crude slabs of concrete on the ground and then hoisted them up and mortared them together. The concrete is rough and unfinished. But this kind of democratic architecture, the simplicity or naivety of this structural system and the liberation that it allows and represents, Kuma goes on to say, was ultimately made possible by the mild and undemanding climate of LA, and by the open space there.

Schindler would continue to make this form of architecture for a time, though eventually, Kuma says, the very climate and space, this lack of external pressure, that had been a kind of liberation, allowed his designs to become safe. He was only capable, Kuma writes, of 'endlessly reproducing the commonplace as commonplace'. It seems, I thought to myself in bed, while thinking at the same time about how I hadn't heard the can or cup being blown up and down the driveway since returning inside, that this applies to art of all kinds, that any eradication or escape from formalism and from the pressures that add and force complication, is likely to be temporary. Any liberation, may well swing us right back to the commonplace.

Yesterday, I installed an exhaust fan in a window of my studio, where I'd accidentally broken the glass by dropping a timber board against it, while a neighbour who lives above us ran back and forth across the car park with a small grey dog I'd never seen before. It just happened that I'd broken the window while the window frames of our block were being painted. After I'd cleared out the broken pieces of glass and covered the opening over with a piece of plywood, I'd told one of the painters about it and he'd replied almost angrily, *who broke it*, as though I'd accused him or one of his workers of doing so. When I'd repeated that it had been me who had broken the window, he'd smiled.

This morning when I returned from a walk, the neighbour who had been running around the car park with a dog was sitting cross-legged on the floor of our kitchen going through three boxes of books that we'd driven to a second-hand store some months ago only to have discovered the store had closed down. This neighbour is a teacher and my partner was standing against the wall heater talking to her about her history classes on the Vietnam War. Last Friday, the neighbour said, the class had been debating whether it would have been acceptable to have fought in any era of the war, whether the fear of the spread of communism was genuine at the beginning, or whether at least one could have been excused for not knowing any better at that time. I started the debate, she said, but then I just found myself telling them that no, none of it was okay. I have to tone it down a bit, she went on, but at least they're learning to argue against me. Beside her, there was a big stack of the books she was intending to take. These are all very grim, she said.

This was the first time this neighbour had ever been in our apartment, despite having lived above us for several years, and I was surprised and a little disappointed that she hadn't been at all curious to see beyond our kitchen.

Red, faded red and royal blue lagoon

arc over circle

a black
steel window frame

the thinness of a bicycle lying on

tall grass

After the tree loppers cut back the ivy that had spread over one end of the roof of the garages of our apartment building, our German neighbour told my partner and me about how the ivy had once grown over the entire back, red brick wall of the apartment building itself. It was magnificent, she said, but found its way into the gutters and the windows. It never stops, she continued. We'd only been living there a few months by then but already I'd noticed small ivy shoots with outsized leaves popping up throughout the garden.

Over time, our German neighbour told us about the people who have moved in and out, how healthy the lawn that has now largely given over to sand had once been, about the lights that had been installed, and about how the low unattractive wall made of sleepers stained a faint copper green was built along the front of the driveway to prevent one particular resident from parking on the grass.

Now when people move in, my partner and I tell them about the stair treads that have been or will soon need to be replaced, the rubbish pulled out from behind the garages, the pets that have come and gone, and the trees that have been cut down or had branches removed.

At the other end of the rear boundary, away from the tall ivy-covered fence, behind the garages, a former resident had dumped sheets of fibre cement. Until recently an orange cat would come through a small opening in the low fence at this end, where we share a boundary with a narrow apartment block. The orange cat and our own cat would lie in the sun in the car park, or on the roof of the garages, always several metres away from each other. Each time you would look up at them, their arrangement would have changed. The orange cat's owner moved away, and now a cat that my partner says has the face of a wolf comes through the opening. I've only seen this cat running across the car park, its tail as wide as its body but, one evening, it had appeared by my partner's feet while she was pulling leaves from the bay tree.

Some weeks after I'd cleared out the other end, I pulled out the fibre cement sheets and dug into the ground, expecting the kind of rubbish I'd found previously. There was some broken glass, which I threw into a bucket, but that seemed to be all. After a while, however, my shovel hit metal, and I dug out what seemed to be the frame of a bench, with two tubular steel legs. The back must have been bolted to the wall. I pulled the frame out into the car park, and could then see that it would have once been painted black or a deep blue, but it had rusted badly. It was the same length, I noticed, as each of the garages are wide. It was likely once bolted against the end wall of one of them.

I've ordered an out-of-print monograph on an artist from three different vendors this week, but each time I've received a cancellation notice saying the book is unavailable. The artist typically creates monochrome paintings, prints and sculptures derived from forms he's come across in the world of made things: a concrete road distance marker on an island off France, a pattern of fenestration, two buildings overlapping, the two arcs and two diverging lines of a flattened paper cup. Today, it seems, my order has finally been accepted.

Seeing the rusted metal frame lying on the asphalt where I'd placed it, I had an image of my father pulling a twisted length of metal guide rail out of a cave. I hadn't thought of this camping trip the two of us had gone on for what seemed like a great many years, but there it was, feeling close and near. We'd camped by a dry creek bed on the edge of a largely emptied-out inland town with a disused tin mine. My father's white t-shirt and white trousers were marked with red from the earth of the caves. At the entrance, he'd thrown the guide rail down over the metal staircase onto the grass.

This afternoon, I came across an article from almost thirty years ago about a group of boys in New York who had entered a storm water system through an entrance that had been left open for several weeks as part of a water mains project. Within the tunnels, two of the boys had gone down a bank and had then found themselves unable to climb back up. They continued on, looking for a way out but then the boy at the front, born the same year as one of my brothers, had suddenly vanished. The second boy turned back and was helped up the bank by his friends with a rope. Officials initially speculated, the article explained, that the boy who'd vanished had found a way out and was hiding out of embarrassment for the commotion he'd caused, but once a map of the system had been obtained, it was clear he'd stepped into a 500-foot-deep lightless shaft.

My father and I had driven down a long straight graded dirt road on the way to the caves and the camping ground. The road passed clusters of old timber buildings. Every so often, a length of a remnant train line would reappear by the road, on a ridge blown over with sand. We stopped and went inside one of the buildings. It was a single room, and had shutters running along a bench built into an outer wall, as though it had been a store. The floor inside was sandy compacted earth, the walls lined with newspaper. 'Fuck off' had been painted across the wall opposite the doorway.

We were in an old grey jeep-like 4WD. The back had a corrugated metal floor, and timber bench seats running front to back along the sides. The vehicle must have belonged to a friend of my father's.

One morning, my father and I drove to the disused tin mine. The mine, or what was left of it, was a long timber building running up the side of a hill. At the base, there was a flat round car park, bordered by a metal chain running between timber posts. The hillside was bare red earth sprayed with dark rocks, many of which had a hardened sea-green foam of lichen on their uppermost points. We followed the path up beside the structure. Stairs had been cut into the earth. Here and there, the red and white metal corrugated roof had collapsed. Some of the boards on the side had been kicked in. We placed our heads in through the gaps. The floor within the near-black interior seemed to be far below the ground we were standing on. It would be full of bats, my father said. He clapped his hands loudly into the space, receiving no response from anything.

This morning I woke early. In the kitchen, I pulled down the blind so that it shot up. There were thick drops of rain, like on a newly waterproofed coat, on the roof of the black car outside the window.

The car's interior was illuminated, and one of my neighbours was sitting in the driver's seat. With the angle, the top half of his head was obscured, though I could see his mouth was moving. Oh, I thought to myself, he's talking. A balcony door was ajar on the upper level of the narrow apartment block behind. A gently moving white curtain was pulled across the opening.

There was, I recalled while having breakfast, another time when my father was driving the grey jeep. The vehicle had been parked on the river rocks amongst low open tea trees with delicate grey foliage. My brother, a friend of mine and I had been walking upstream beside the river through the trees, over rocks and stepping into soft sand, and then floating down the glassy rapids. Only this friend had, on our final go, not brought himself in towards the bank in time and had been pulled down to the concrete bridge, where he'd clung to a pillar. My father had rushed up onto the bridge, and my brother and I were soon on either side of him, waiting to grab at my friend once my father had pulled him within our reach. I could see through the rapids that one of my friend's black sneakers had come off.

The water at the campsite had a strong mineral taste. It tastes, my father said, like I've cut my lip. It's oddly pleasant, he said. There was one other camper at the site, set up at the centre of the grounds by a ring of large poinciana and flame trees. While we were washing our breakfast bowls under the tap, the man came over to us and said we should see the yabbies in the creek bed. Carrying a blue bucket, the man took us down past the first bend, and there they were, five or six of them, huddled together in what appeared to be the last puddle of water. My father and I had walked down through the dry sandy bed the day before, collecting loofahs in a plastic shopping bag. Some of the loofahs still retained their brittle dark outer shell, some didn't. Eventually, we'd come across, in the creek bed, amongst a ring of large rocks, a fire site along with an unrolled sleeping bag and a blue and white styrofoam cooler. Let's go back, my father had said. We hadn't noticed the puddle and the yabbies. What do you think, the man said, can we eat them. Of course, my father replied, kneeling down and trying to grab at one.

I cannot recall my friend finally being pulled up onto the bridge, and I cannot make the scene or series of images work. My friend, my brother and I are either too large or too small in relation to my father. My friend's chest scrapes up the side of the bridge, but then I cannot force his body to bend around the lip. As he's being pulled upward, his face is expressionless, empty of relief or amusement or concern. Perhaps my father had let him go, leaving him to travel beneath the bridge, though he would have had to remain under until he was through, as the water was almost as high as the underside of the structure.

Later by the river, my friend long out of the water, my father made damper batter with rose water and cardamom. We wrapped the batter around the ends of sticks to roast in the fire. Once hardened, we pulled the hollow charred lengths of bread away from the sticks. The hollows we filled with honey.

Just now while digging a clump of clivia out from beneath the tap at the front of the building, I came across a handful of small white glass mosaics with tiny ink-like black dots through them, three orange hose fittings of various ages, an earring made of a marble coiled with wire, and a small piece of clear plastic with the number five written on it in black marker.

After we climbed out of the creek bed, the man asked if I wanted to carry the bucket of yabbies. The spines of their antennas reached out over the rim. I took the handle, holding it up and away from me as we walked. The man said, I'm John, by the way. Ant, my father said, shaking his hand. John was just travelling around, going here, going there. Probably over to Alice next, he said. The two of them discussed the caves near the campsite. A few weeks earlier, John said, he'd been fishing off a jetty over a river at a community at this end of the tablelands. He used to have friends there, he said. A man who had been fishing beside him told him about a cave carved into the hillside not far from there that Chinese miners must have lived in. That afternoon, the man had driven John out of the community and down a dirt road, through the hills to the cave. My father asked John if he'd know how to find it again.

Back at the campsite, John said to me, fill the bucket up at the tap, but not all the way, or they'll climb out. He sat at the table under a shelter and drew a map. When I walked over to them, John ran his pen back and forth over a section of his drawing and said, this hill here is incredibly steep. You'll want to floor it, he said. If you're not going to do that, I wouldn't even try, he went on, looking over at the jeep.

Yesterday the monograph on the artist arrived. He spent the latter half of his twenties, in the late forties and early fifties, in Paris. Later he wrote, you could approach anyone, no matter who they were. Someone had said to him, Picasso was waiting in his car wanting to meet him, this new American. He felt he mustn't go, and didn't. But on a train, he recognised an older artist he admired and introduced himself. The man had asked him to describe one of his works. When he was done, the older man said, what he'd described wasn't art. You cannot, he went on, set out a painting and then fill it in, as he was doing. You have to approach each touch of the canvas with absolute uncertainty, with the knowledge that you are about to make or ruin the work, that you are pushing the work forward while holding it indefinitely together.

The younger artist said to himself, I cannot talk to him. It would be another ten years, he wrote, before he would again be willing to describe his practice to anyone, in speech or in writing. During those ten years, when starting on a new work, he would say to himself, you can't say anything, but you can say each work defines and brings about the terms of its own engagement. This clumsy incantation, he wrote, filled the air with unquiet static.

That evening, John dropped the live yabbies into a pot of boiling water hanging over the campsite fire. We stayed by the fire after we ate, John and my father talking. After a while, my father said I should go to the phone booth to call my mother. I walked down over to the lit-up orange phone box by the road. Once inside, however, I saw that the bottom half of the handset had been smashed away. How, I wondered. The cord didn't reach the concrete base of the booth. I returned briefly to the fire and then climbed into our tent to sleep.

For a while, John and my father spoke quietly in what sounded like an indistinct murmur from inside the tent. Gradually, however, as I fell in and out of sleep, the volume returned to their voices. I would like more than anything, I heard John say suddenly clearly, to go camping with my children, but I've given up trying. All three of them, the younger two following the eldest, have become so resistant, he said. Sometimes, my father said, I would like a little more resistance, to be able to come out here alone like you. When I next woke, my father was telling John about travelling through and working as a draftsman in Iraq and Afghanistan before he'd had children. I'd seen the tan and reddish photographs, the empty site and construction shots mixed in with those of people and temples, all stored in a shallow black leather suitcase.

Yesterday, my partner had the dark ebony piano she'd played through her childhood moved here from her mother's house, where it had sat for the last ten or so years in front of a bookshelf in the shadowy carpeted front room. My partner supervised the move at each end. The only thing that had been on the shelf behind the piano, she said later in the evening, was a child's pencil case that she couldn't recognise. The piano is sleek and rectilinear and is now in the corner of our bedroom where there is a great deal of sunlight in the afternoon. Since the move, the second natural key from the left, the second deepest, has been soundless. When she presses that key down, she said this morning, she feels the air being pulled from her.

I awoke early the following morning at the campsite. My father beside me was still asleep, his face, in the dull light, tinted the green of the tent. My mother, I thought, wakes early. I'd noticed another phone booth outside a store further down the road, beyond a bridge.

I'll call her now, I said to myself, taking my torch and the two twenty cent pieces I'd taken to the phone the night before from a small mesh pocket beside me. I slid out of the tent and pulled on my shoes. They were damp with dew. I walked across the wet grass away from the creek bed towards the road, and then followed the reflective white broken line along its high centre.

A short way down the road, I came across a walking track leading to the network of caves. There was a timber frame, seemingly heavily weathered beneath a recent coat of white paint, over the track to mark the entranceway. Next to the frame, there was a signboard with a map of the network. I looked further down the road towards the bridge and had a sudden image of a child of five or six jumping off it into a river below, but it must have been, I thought, some other bridge. There was no water here.

The hill above the caves was marked with grass-like plants. As I stood looking at the map, I saw there was a man jogging towards me on the edge of the road. He was wearing lime green running shorts, cutting up high at the sides, and a white cotton singlet from a fun run that had been held ten years prior in a town on the tablelands. Beneath the text on the singlet, there was a simple drawing of an echidna, upright, on its hind legs, as though it were jogging. As the man passed, he nodded. He had a Walkman clipped onto the elastic waistband of his shorts, but the headphones were around his neck.

I woke this morning thinking of a hard plastic He Man shampoo bottle I'd had as a child, and something pale blue, red and dark blue that I couldn't quite make out. I'd dreamt my partner and I were being driven around this city in a taxi, only there was nowhere we wanted to go. In the dream, the city was unrecognisable. It was greener, and surrounded by mountains.

When the jogger disappeared into the camber of the road, I thought, I'll call my mother later, and started down the walking track towards the network of caves. The track was gravel and sand, and on both sides there was a low consistent wiry scrub with soft green foliage. Before long, at the foot of the hills, the track opened out to a flat gravel expanse. When we'd been here two days earlier, we'd approached by a different track, but there on the grass next to gravel, like an infant's scribble, was the twisted steel handrail that my father had pulled from a section within.

Earlier today, while taking the compost out to the drums down the side of the garages, I stopped by the planters in the far corner of the car park that are overrun with a type of parsley that has a far broader and bitterer leaf that the parsley we originally planted and picked up a tennis ball from the leaflitter. Half of the ball was a pale creamy yellow from the sun. I threw it downward to bounce, but the ball stayed dead on the ground. When I picked it up again, I could feel the pieces of cracked rubber skeleton moving against each other beneath the felt. I threw the ball up high, aiming for it to arc into an empty terracotta pot on the far side of the car park, but I missed by a long way, the ball going both far and wide, hitting the end wall before disappearing behind a small shrub next to a lemon tree. A moment later, the ball reappeared and began slowly rolling back down across the asphalt towards me. Watching its descent, as it passed one after another of the white parking lines, I silently urged it on. When it reached me, I picked it up and again threw it towards the terracotta pot, but again I missed, far and wide. This time, however, the ball never reappeared.

I'd been feeling aimless, like a child, all morning. I looked down at the black disc from where the ball had been removed from the leaflitter. What to do next, I asked myself. As I picked up the compost bin, I had the feeling of standing beside a friend who I haven't spoken to in several years, while on the coast of Portugal, looking far down into a near perfect circle of hard blue ocean where a cylinder of rocky coastline had long ago fallen in. Travelling together had felt like a mistake, but it was more likely, I thought as I emptied the compost into the black drum, that the discomfort I'd been experiencing was that of having newly stepped out of a kind of cusp-of-adulthood in-between time, out of an easy pleasure of not needing to know anyone or anything, a romance of apartness, marklessness.

I climbed the steel mesh flight of stairs to the opening of the cave and turned around and looked back towards the road, but it was concealed by the contours of the ground, and the scrub. I could see the red poincianas and flame trees around the campsite in the distance. A little way into the cave, I had to get onto my hands and knees and crawl. As the passage narrowed, I took the torch from my pocket and turned it on. Soon, the tunnel opened onto a large cavern. I'd expected, when my father and I had made our way here previously, to see stalactites reaching down towards us, but instead the ceiling here billowed with what looked like encrusted salt. Again, I ran my torch over the folds of the ceiling. A planet, I thought. Suddenly terrified, I said to myself, count to twenty and you'll be okay. At ten I turned off the torch and then at twenty I felt better and turned it on again.

The work the artist had described to the older man had been a series of chimney structures from around Paris in solid blocks of blue and green on a white background, as though their buildings had vanished around them.

At the far side of the cavern, I climbed a metal ladder to the opening from where my father had pulled the twisted section of metal handrail. I hadn't followed him into this passage and he hadn't gone far himself, finding it too narrow. I again crawled on my hands and knees and then briefly on my belly before the passage became tall enough for me to stand and walk. Further along, to the left, there was a waist-height smaller entrance that had been chained off, though the chain had been pulled away from one side. I lifted myself up and into the tunnel. It was low and I was soon crawling on my belly once more. The floor was smooth and glass-like. There was no way, I realised a short way in, I'd be able to turn around.

This afternoon while I was washing dishes, a neighbour ran across the car park to the clothesline. She quickly pulled her white and blue sheets down, bundling them into her arms, before racing back, huddled over her washing, across the car park. By then, it had been raining steadily for half an hour. There's something incredibly joyous, I thought to myself, about seeing someone frantically retrieving washing from a clothesline in the rain.

I crawled further into the cave, my torch pointed forward, hoping to reach an area where I could turn around. Eventually, I came to a point where the floor seemed to drop away. I pulled myself forward so that my shoulders and head hung over the drop and pointed my torch downward. I thought, if it's not too deep, I'll climb in, turn around and climb out again, only it was difficult to make sense of the hole. There seemed to be ground just there, but also no ground at all. It'll be fine, I thought, I'll just lower myself, and if I don't reach the ground, I'll climb back out. But, I thought, I'll have to lower myself head first. I took one of the twenty cent pieces from my pocket and let it fall. There was nothing. The surface must be sand, I thought, and then, from far below, I heard the coin chiming against rock. I forced myself backwards through the narrow passage, wanting to be nowhere near the depth of the hole. Patches of the top of the tunnel, I now realised, were likewise encrusted with what looked like salt. With my shirt pulled up from the backward movement, the floor of the cave felt cool, almost wet. Again, I started to panic. I turned my torch off and again started counting. It's so quiet, I thought, I could be in a cylinder falling through space. I laid my head down, my cheek against the rock or glass or metal.

Earlier today, I stood towards the centre of a full, hot tram heading into the city, reading an essay about an artist who, the author wrote, wants his sculptures to be pure spatial experiences. There is always a tension, the author wrote, in the artist's work between appealing to memory, and the ideal of blocking out and suffocating anything exterior. The author quoted the sculptor as saying, once an artist develops a language, they should remain always within that language.

Last night while I was watering plants around our car park, the cat with a face of a wolf walked across the top of the brick wall, that's five or six metres high, between us and next door, with heavy clouds behind, his pale body illuminated by the spotlight beside the bay tree.

My father reversed away from the steep incline, stopped and then said, well, and accelerated quickly. Near the top, the vehicle slowed. Don't, my father said, but then we crested the hill. From here we could see down into the valley of trees and white-grey boulders sprayed with orange lichen. My father parked, turned the car off and stretched his hands out above the wheel. We walked over to the outcrop of boulders that John had marked on the map. From here, we could see that the boulders ran all the way down the side of the mountain. We were much higher than I'd realised. Further down, it looked as though you could jump from one boulder to the next.

When we came to the gap between the rocks that needed to be jumped to cross to the cave, my father said, ha. He looked down into the gap. Of course, he said, but I guess you just have to. He took a few steps back and leapt across. He then dragged out a plank of wood that John had mentioned to slide across the gap. He walked back over to my side and said, do it quickly, one, two steps. I'd rather jump, I said, but then I stepped across.

This cave was only as deep as a living room. The rock floor was smooth from wear. At the far end, where the cave narrowed and became lower, there was a timber beam across its width, with planks running back from the beam to a shelf carved into the rear wall to make a kind of loft bed. Chinese characters had been carved all the way along the beam. My father ran his hand over the timber, over the characters. Think what it would be like, he said, coming all this way, not having any idea what to expect and then ending up here in this cave, seemingly nowhere on the side of a mountain. Someone had recently had a fire towards the centre of the cave. I'd thought we would be able to spend the night here, my father said, but we can't possibly. I crawled to the outermost ledge and hung my head over and looked down at the cascade of orange and silver boulders.

This morning, returning from a walk I came across a dead female blackbird at the front of our building, below the sunroom window of the neighbour who I'd seen pulling washing from the clothesline. I'd often watched the male and the female blackbird busying through the leaflitter by our driveway, and darting weightlessly along our fence. Immediately, I retrieved a shovel and buried the bird beside a small grey tea tree that I planted only months ago. I did not want to see the bird again.

My cat
does not understand
why her stomach
has been
shaved
cut
and folded

When I tried to
move her out
from the carrier
she made a
crying shrieking
sound that
I've never before
heard her
make

We removed
the top of the
carrier
and put it
next to the
heater

The vet
had not been able
to take it all
out

She would have
had to, she said,
make a much
bigger incision, and to
have cut away one of her
ribs entirely

She said, we'll see
what pathology says
but I
don't think it's
going to be
nice

I am
on the bed near her
watching Father of
the Bride 2 crying

I awoke this morning saying to myself a few disconnected lines from a song, about it being so long ago, and it now being just a dream, and yet it feeling so real. I recognised the lines as being from a John Lennon song, though not one that I believed, lying there, that I'd previously thought about, or had ever really noticed. I thought, it's likely that he's singing about his time in the Beatles. I tried then to think of a Beatles song, but I couldn't. I could just see black and white footage of two of them—John and Paul, I thought—simultaneously and symmetrically moving closer and then further away from a microphone. The two of them seemed to be shimmering with minute vibrations, as though there was a running motor beneath the stage they were standing on. It was, I thought, dream-like.

Last night I watched part of a French film about two men staying in a big house by the sea. Throughout the part that I watched, one of the men was wearing a straw-coloured button-up shirt with the sleeves rolled up and the top few buttons undone, loose tailored black trousers and black espadrilles. The other man had a big red terry-towelling robe wrapped loosely around him. They discussed, at length, how they intended to do nothing, to not even think, during their stay in the house. The man wearing espadrilles said that it's in his nature to do nothing. The man in the robe replied, but it's easier to resist your nature than to go with it. He then said that he'd seen the other man reading, and that reading is not doing nothing. But, the man in the espadrilles said, it's better to give my thoughts over to a book, to move through a book unthinkingly, than to think my own thoughts.

It seemed odd to me, lying there in bed, that in order to evoke the dream-like quality of the memory, the song had to emphasise how conversely real the memory had felt. In my state of half wakefulness, I couldn't think how else this could have been done.

This morning I started rereading the Peter Handke novel *Short Letter, Long Farewell*. On his first night in America, the narrator finishes reading *The Great Gatsby*. The following day, he steps outside and says aloud to himself, this is my second day in America. Speaking aloud to himself is something he hasn't done since he was a child, when he did it so as to not feel as though he were alone. When he first did it, the night before when he arrived at the hotel, he couldn't stop giggling. That morning, as he stepped out of the hotel, he thought, now, being in America and having finished the book, or having so recently emerged from it, he would be renewed. He would take on the characteristics he'd discovered in *The Great Gatsby*. Only, he said to himself, there would be nowhere for him to present these characteristics because he'd left his old environment behind. In this environment, he said to himself, he could only be someone who rode on buses, used public conveniences, drank in bars and stayed in hotels.

The man wearing the red terry-towelling robe said that people who think too much aren't alive or, perhaps he said, they don't exist. We only have two or three original thoughts, he said, in a lifetime, if that. I recalled, while watching the film, that a lecturer once said this very thing to my class. The lecture theatre we were in was small and dark and always felt almost perfectly round or globe-like, even though all of the walls were themselves flat. There were no windows in the theatre, but somehow you were always aware that the building was right up next to a large park that ran between the campus and the river, around the perimeter of which were great big strangler figs. I recalled wondering whether the originality of a thought mattered, and whether, if it did, you would get to the original thoughts by way of unoriginal thoughts, or whether they would suddenly appear. How, I thought, would we recognise them, know them, and how would you stop the impulse to suppress them, hold them down. I thought, could there be no pleasure in thought alone. Or rather, could we not rediscover the pleasure in thought. Was our desire to stop it, to curtail it, to drown it with clean, blank spaciousness, the very thing that made thought feel so unpleasant, so stream-like, so pointlessly voluminous.

A few evenings ago, I read an article on the early German sociologist Max Weber. Weber wrote, the article explained, that the protestant sanctification of earthly pursuits had laid the groundwork for the coming of capitalism, which, in time, eventually supplanted more or less entirely the idea that we derive meaning from religion. Now, Weber said, each of us had to derive and maintain our own meaning.

The unpleasantness of thought is perhaps just its accumulation. Temporal depth, the feeling of existing through time, of being buttressed by time may be in a way pleasant, or reassuring—it counters or staves off the feeling of being in a continuous vacuous present that is quickly dematerialising—but the idea of a single long stream of unbroken thought is frightening, trap-like. One wants to cut or push breaks into it, submerge large sections of it, to create definition.

Last night in bed, I tried to recall who it was who had spoken about the small but crucial difference between having the ability to weather adversity and having the ability to weather the experience of being knocked around by that adversity. Was it, I wondered, a friend, or my partner, or had it been someone on a podcast, or a character in a book.

I have been waking in the middle of the night trapped in long persistent streams of thought, or simply sensations. One of the sensations was linked to walking through a large, endless industrial Atlantic port city on the border of France and Spain, ducking under a high chain-link fence and walking along a long stretch of seemingly unused asphalt covered in gravel with the dark ocean straight ahead in the distance.

So often sleeping badly, I can never feel as though consciousness is sustained, singular and ongoing. After a few nights of sleeping well, I feel renewed, but I also feel, in my wakefulness, a hard break with the now unreachable days immediately preceding. Or, perhaps, I'm made aware of the way consciousness never can be continuous, that we cannot hold it all.

I was walking through this border city with a friend. Days earlier, we'd walked through a village that looked as though it hadn't changed for centuries. We'd filled our water bottles in an icy stone fountain, and had then walked down to the river to eat. Afterwards, I napped in the sun, sliding in and out of sleep, while my friend kicked around in the stony river bank and said, I just want to find something old.

Wasn't Nelson killed, the woman asks the man
who is showing her around the hall.

Yes, he says, but we still won.

Her husband is being told that the body of the woman he was
hiking through the Swiss Alps with, some fifty years earlier,
who fell through a fissure into a glacier below,
has been found.

like some Second World War pilots

Climate change has melted the snow and ice.

In Italy an entire barracks has popped
right out into the open, with preserved spirit lamps,
diaries and timber crates.

He can hardly catch a bus into town.

deeply hurt by his distraction.

an atlas, a cabin

he's taken of her the morning before she fell

Confronting him, the wife says,

when there's happiness,

having to maintain a wholeness,
an intactness,
the idea

of what the relationship is, has always been,

until there is an end
without time for

another

In an essay I read earlier today, an English author writes that the blue uniform her two children wear to school identifies them in time and place the same way Victorian dress or Roman togas did. She writes that her children, who, day after day, leave and come and leave and come home in their blue uniforms, have a neutrality about them that seems to suggest they are patiently awaiting an answer.

Last night I dreamt that my partner and I were at a restaurant that was owned by an old friend of mine who I haven't seen for over fifteen years. The old friend sat down at our table and tried, for the first time, her restaurant's four cheese pizza. The cheese on the pizza was a deep orange.

Later, a group of us walked through a city that was this city and then was Tokyo. The old friend and I held hands and discussed having children. I had a sense she was going to say something comforting about my partner and I not having them, but instead she said of my partner, who was now walking ahead of us, she's become so intelligent.

This morning, I wheeled a thick black tubular steel eighties or nineties dining table frame that had been on the side of the road a few blocks to our apartment building. Sitting perpendicular to the trolley, which tends to weave from side to side, the frame was too wide to push along the footpath. Most of the way, I had to wheel it down the high centre part of the road. I felt gently and pleasantly elated moving the table, and when I passed a woman pushing two children in a pram in the other direction, it felt as though we ought to acknowledge each other. The woman, however, looked away.

Yesterday, I finished reading Sheila Heti's autobiographical novel *Motherhood.* The narrator, who reads as Heti herself, discusses the volume of time we spend churning over decisions that, in some sense, we have little control over anyhow. It's comforting, she says, to structure and plan a future, but doing so doesn't necessarily have any bearing on that future.

A poet on a podcast I was listening to earlier today said that although she's always loved the confessional poets and although she must have read and reread three or four or more of Plath's and Sexton's and Lowell's and whoever else's books every year for the past thirty or so years, she can never write it herself. To confess on the page, she said, you have to be somehow exalted, to have somewhere to fall. I've never felt, she said, that I could plummet any further.

At work today, a colleague told me that she and her husband would jokingly refer to their cat to their only daughter as her sister. Please stop calling her my sister, the daughter said to them a few days ago, I don't want a sister.

Last night over dinner, a friend of ours said that he'd been afraid of owning a dog because he'd heard how distraught people can be when they lose them. Their lives, he said, are much shorter than ours. He and his partner had, a few months earlier, become the owners of a two-year-old staffy cross, Lily. During the evening, Lily barked and growled at my partner and me whenever we neared.

On the Saturday morning just passed, a friend came around to paint a set of Windsor chairs I'd found for her apartment. The chairs had spent the last few months in my garage. Seeing them again, I thought they were awful. My head was throbbing. The joints of one of the chairs were loose, so I knocked them apart, but while doing so, a spindle from the backrest shattered. I wanted nothing to do with the chairs, and my head continued to throb. I went inside and laid down on our bed, leaving my friend outside in the courtyard, painting.

In bed last night, my partner said Lily was the first dog to ever growl at her. I didn't want to show it, she said, but I was terrified.

Reading Heti's *Motherhood,* I thought about how much I once enjoyed making plans with friends, regardless of whether the plans were likely to eventuate. I had planned, along with a friend who now lives with her two children on an island south of this city, to visit a beach in Ireland with black sand. Later, another friend and I had planned to ride from here to a city far in the north along the train line. We had taken the train north during a university break and had watched the dirt track that ran beside the line for as much of the journey as we could, planning how we would cross rivers and find food and water.

At the end of Heti's novel the narrator says that reaching the end of her childbearing years is a great relief, that possibilities seem to suddenly open up. It's like, she says, a second childhood. As well as the freedom of not having children, she's experiencing the sudden compression of time. There can seem as though there's so much of it to work through when you're younger, so many distracting and apparent opportunities.

This afternoon, while retrieving a plywood sheet from our garage, a large heavy glass tabletop slipped from my hand and shattered against a drafting stool. I spent the next few hours carefully cleaning up the glass, picking it out of the furniture stored in there. The rosewood and steel frame that the glass top belonged to is stamped with the name of a Brazilian architect, and while I've come across images online of a matching lounge chair of his, I've never come across this table, so it remains in my mind the only one of its kind. After the glass had been cleared away, I was devastated. What now, I wondered, to do with this frame.

In an interview, Gertrude Stein says that in Cézanne's work, compositionally, one thing has as much weight as the next. Each part, she says, in his work is as important as the whole, and that impresses me enormously.

Last night I dreamt I was driving through the streets of Manila, where I have never been. The streets were laid with pale bluish concrete and, after a parade, I was to meet an old friend I'd run into several years ago outside a bookstore. I stopped the car behind a van to look at three chairs on the side of the road. They were timber and canvas sling chairs with a complicated design. Even though a man was sitting on one of them, I couldn't understand how to sit down.

Around fifteen years ago, I woke one morning in a bright red tent within the ramparts of the old town of Carcassonne. I'd arrived by train late the night before and had walked through the unlit streets looking for somewhere to stay or camp. When I unzipped the tent that morning, a doberman raced over, snarling and barking fiercely, its face the same height as mine. Over the sound of the dog I could hear the owner screaming. I then watched from beside my tent as the owner pounded the dog with his fists on the sandy gravel, the beautiful castle that I was seeing in the sunlight for the first time behind.

The narrator of Shirley Hazzard's *The Bay of Noon* mentions that a centenarian had told her that 'memory protects one from the burden of experience'. The centenarian had gone on to say that all she could remember of five or six years around the turn of the century was the dress that someone wore and the colour of a curtain. The narrator says she herself would be pleased to remember Naples in such a way, by the lilac dress worn by a dear friend one morning on a drive, or the sienna-coloured curtain in one of her apartments.

The gardener has cut the outermost edge away from the delicate pale green-grey saltbush by our car park. You can see the arcing shadow of what's been removed on the asphalt, and the fine lifeless network within.

This afternoon while I was carrying furniture that I would likely never fix out of my garage to the nature strip, a quiet, attractive electrician in his mid-thirties who lives in one of the ground floor apartments said, oh, has somebody booked hard rubbish. Yes, I said, for the twelfth. Right, he said, the twelfth, we have some time then. But, his French partner said, we don't have anything we need to get rid of. No, he said, we don't. But, if we do, he said, we'll put it out by the twelfth.

'But memory,' Hazzard's narrator continues, 'at an interval of only fifteen years, is less economical and less poetic, still clouded with effects that seemed to be their causes. The search is still underway in unlikely places—too assiduous; too far from home.'

This afternoon while we were visiting our neighbour Kelly in her apartment, I thought the rain must be getting in, but then I realised the soft tapping sound I could hear was drumming on the radio.

Yesterday my partner and I had lunch at her mother's house. When we arrived, her mother stood outside on the driveway holding her caramel-coloured toy poodle puppy, Mica. I took hold of Mica, who squirmed in my arms and flapped her forearms against my face. After lunch, my partner and her mother took Mica for a walk.

While they were out, I stood in the back garden, under a Japanese maple and phoned my mother. She was staying with my sister, in a town well north of here. My sister had moved there a year ago, but my mother hadn't yet told me the name of the town. The brother of my sister's former partner, the father of her child, my mother had said, works at a telecommunications company, and he finds things out that he couldn't otherwise know.

Now on the phone, I asked if the second syllable of the town's name was the name of an animal. No, what do you mean, she said. I said the name of the town I'd guessed. Oh, she said, well, yes, close. My sister, she said, had been doing well. She was working at a leisure centre. A kind neighbour had bought her son a scooter. I think she's liked having me here, she said.

My mother told me that a friend of my sister's had sold them a car that my mother had driven to the small town for my sister to use. The friend, she went on, had said that the car might very occasionally skip gear. But, she said, it happens all the time and out of every gear, out of third, out of fourth. I just had to let go, she said, and tell myself that it was time. She'd stopped at a friend's house on the way to deliver some pots, and when she'd stepped out of the car she'd been shaking. I asked her why she hadn't simply turned back. Well, she replied, I couldn't, could I.

I mentioned that I'd been reading the journals of William Dampier. I believe they found a plaque of his on the north west coast, she said. Perhaps, I said, I'm not sure. She asked the name of his ship. I said, the Roebuck, but at the moment he's jumping from ship to ship, anything they can get on. I said I wasn't sure I'd continue with it. I said, I know I should just face it, but there are so many pages describing manatees and turtles and monkeys being caught and killed. Yes, she said, they would just go to an island and wipe things out. People too, she said.

I shouldn't be surprised by this, I said, but you can sense by the way he describes, say, a manatee, its lips, its eyes, its movement, how moved he is by its beauty, and then in the next sentence he's discussing the texture of its flesh. It doesn't seem, I said, as though that had been a difficult transition for him to have made.

When my partner and her mother returned from the walk my partner said they'd stopped to sit on a bench in a park and an elderly man had approached. He'd stood a few metres away from them looking at Mica. My partner said she'd asked the man if he'd had a dog. The man hadn't responded. He'd just closed his eyes.

This morning when I opened my laptop to work, it was out of power. The lead was in the bedroom where my partner was still sleeping. My cat came and sat down on the curve of the sofa's arm beside me, a curve that fits her perfectly, and where she's left shadowy marks. I wasn't yet sufficiently awake to read so decided to listen to music on my iPod. Most of the music on there I haven't listened to for several years and the only thing I could face was an album by an American folk musician about the death of his wife from cancer. Towards the beginning of the first track, he mentions a package arriving addressed to his wife, who had passed away a few days earlier. In the package there's a backpack she's ordered for their baby daughter to take to school in a few years' time. This line more than anything makes me want to have a child.

Sun and heat
deep in the capillaries
of your sedimentary fur
that, holding you down, I
rip from you with a steel comb

Gertrude Stein
is both warning and
clarion
A lesson that refuses
to teach
She is claws cut
out and held
A sequence of waves
that remain
at equal distance from
one another
as they traverse a great
expanse
A cul-de-sac
with one last inhabited house

Language and its
unsteady forward movement
its liquid pull
against simultaneity

Daily, I visit the grotty inner cove of your ear

After Gauguin and Van Gogh cut each
other's ears off with fencing
sabres they shot each
other

Gauguin would go on to have
two children. He was the better
artist

Sometimes the better artist survives the lesser
artist

Would it be better
I ask myself
to be
thankful

I flick through a book about a Norwegian aritst and, of his works,
think, I like this one, I don't like this one, I like this one. The ones
I like are roughly painted, at times so much so that you can see
the white of the canvas beneath. The ones I don't like have swirls
around people's

heads

In any case the
following year the
Nazis invaded the
south of
France

What came next, abstract expressionism, is misleadingly named. It does not abstract, does not derive from. All Western non-decorative artwork up until this point had in various ways abstracted from the physical world. Abstraction is recognised in its absence. It could, perhaps, be seen as a reversal of abstraction; where previously the artist pulled out from the world towards the work, or had run the world of things through their own being and consciousness, abstract expressionism allows or leaves the viewer to find relatedness, to pull towards. Jackson Pollock was now read as dancer and boxer. He was the masculine who, in the physicalisation of expression and by painting on canvases that, in their enormity, restrained his impulse towards composition, denied himself control of connotation and literal meaning, or the sense that there could be such a thing, thereby, in a way, silencing

himself

or bringing all into silence

You couldn't say everything so

you said

nothing

The yellow, orange and pink

poppies

in a vase on the

dining room table

have been

dropping petals all

morning

Or abstract

expressionism or

certain versions of it

becomes about the individual expression of the mark: the singularity of one's mark and the way the mark speaks, or speaks for us. This was a move from how one sees to how one gestures. One can imagine a series of artists' strokes, one beside the other, through which we could feel and compare their personhood, a possibility

parodied or in some way commented on

by Roy Lichtenstein's 'White Brushstroke', a

cartoon-like recreation of a

roughly textured streak of white

paint

It was discovered recently that Van

Gogh painted tree

roots

'I don't ask my students to choose, but every

last one of them

does.'

By now we know that not only do

eggs and bottles not have to look like

eggs and bottles

but

they don't need to be painted at

all

This morning, in my neighbour Kelly's apartment, I read a poem based on a character from an eighteenth century novel who, after being shipwrecked, spent much of his life stranded on an island.

I was in Kelly's apartment to feed and spend time with her cat, who spends much of the day either as a lump under the blankets or hiding from me under the bed. This morning, after I put her food down, I walked into the hallway, and there she was. I stopped and bent slowly down and she hissed at me, once more, with astonishing commitment and hatred.

In the poem, the man on the island wishes he had some form of kettle.

A few weeks ago, we sold our couch, having put another on layby at a twentieth-century modern furniture store, a couch that we can barely afford. The living room now feels wonderfully empty and without structure. It feels as though you could live without similarity from day to day, even though we rarely sat on the couch.

I've been trying, increasingly, to imagine myself somewhere where I can, for instance, walk or swim in the early morning in an environment that feels untouched. While out walking near where we live, I'll weigh attractive aspects against the ugly, trying to decide finally if we're in the right place. But, I find myself then thinking, the natural, the seemingly untouched, and the conceptual effort to separate this out, is only another reminder of our destructiveness. Besides, I find myself thinking, I cannot justify turning away from the types of environment that we ourselves are responsible for creating.

Earlier today as I was going out, our German neighbour rushed from her kitchen door onto the landing to tell me that there was a pigeon nesting in a cardboard box outside an apartment on the top floor. She said she didn't know if the box had intentionally been left out for the pigeon. The first time my neighbour had gone up there, the pigeon had seemed not to mind her, but then the second time it had flapped around angrily. When she'd gone a third time, the pigeon hadn't been there, so she'd placed a sheet of cardboard over the box. But later again, the piece of cardboard was gone and the pigeon was once again in the box.

On the bus to work today, I listened to a poetry podcast reading. Describing the poem he was about to read, the poet said, there is nothing as beautiful as an empty freshly painted room, without, he said, your lunch or your dry cleaning. Then, he said, you bring in one chair, and then you bring in another.

On the bus, I noticed someone had spray painted along the top of a building: Cola World Cola World Cola World Cola World Cola World.

Just now, I curled around our cat, who was sleeping on our bed, her butterfly ear flapping in my too-near face. How many couples, I wondered, are held together by the limitless love and affection they're about to pour into an animal.

In my neighbour's apartment this morning, I took a book-length interview with a philosopher and novelist who had a shock of silver hair from the shelf. It's arbitrary, she says, to connect sex and love. Though, she says, she could never desire anyone she doesn't love, and couldn't love anyone she isn't going to remain with for many years.

Earlier today, while I was taking tools and other things back out to my studio from our apartment, our German neighbour called out to me. She'd been woken at 5am by the pigeon. She doesn't have any idea, she said, how the other tenants cope. She'd gone up there and shooed the pigeon away and inside the box there had been another pigeon that was dead and covered in maggots. There were so many flies, she said, moving her arms around to portray the mass of flies.

Later, the philosopher and novelist with a shock of silver hair said that she'd always been wary of metaphors. She realised very young, she said, that when people demonstrate something with a metaphor that something else entirely could have be said, or proven, if a different metaphor had been chosen.

Yesterday, at the bookstore where I work, a woman asked where she can find the books about people who go to France and fall in love. Later, at the counter, she said, there used to be many more of these books. I asked her if she would be interested in a novel that was similar. Yes, she said, I know what you mean.

After work, I checked my phone. My partner had texted to say I'd left the stove on. You could have killed our cat, she wrote, stop doing this. The water in the kettle, I thought, must have boiled away hours ago. All day, the kettle would have been making that unplaceable ticking sound.

I spent much of this morning reading in Kelly's apartment. Our apartment is on the ground floor, hers is up in the canopy of the trees. The screen of variegated leaves forms a light-porous soft green curtain across the entirety of her sunroom and living room windows.

The neighbours who live above Kelly's apartment are both musicians who freelance across orchestras and teach. One of them plays the cello, the other the double bass. They practise in their apartment, as the double bassist was doing for much of the morning. The music was slow and reedy and comforting. Their practising, however, drives Kelly mad, being so constant and repetitive.

Last night, trying to fall asleep, I thought about the ways the man on the island could have made a kettle, whether he could have, for instance, dug up clay and built a small kiln. I wondered if he could have slowly heated water in the shell of a coconut or in a vessel carved out of timber hung clear of the flames.

The expensive sofa from the twentieth-century modern furniture store arrived today. It had looked compact in the open space of the shop, but is far too large for our living room. In any case, when I removed the cushions to pull it out into a daybed, I noticed a crack running the entire length of the base.

Last night, our cat jumped onto the bentwood chair that's tucked into a table in our second bedroom with a smoked glass surface and a rosewood and metal frame. She watched from below as I slid my hand across and tabletop and as I pushed my face down against the glass.

A few months ago, Kelly borrowed my audio sampler to record the neighbours above her practising, as well as walking around noisily in boots, and the man's loud pissing. She said, it's not her job to tell him to piss on the side of the bowl. The night before she left, when she gave me the key and outlined how to look after her cat, she returned the recorder. She said she'd made the recordings but hadn't listened to them. I've now saved them in a folder on my desktop, but haven't listened to them either.

A man in the bookstore I work in said to a colleague of mine a few days ago, this is the second time today someone's given me exactly $1.10 in change. Later I became annoyed at a woman for unwrapping a children's book that has a great many loose pieces inside. I said, how do we sell this now? She looked at me blankly and said, I don't know.

When I went up to feed Kelly's cat last night, there was a wasp flying around her bathroom. I gently trapped it with a tissue up against the glass of the sash window. The window has a circular ventilation fan installed in its centre, and was open at the bottom the small amount the fan would allow, and was screened on the outside. There was a line of dead bees covered in a fine tan dust along the base of the screen. I left the room and dropped the tissue along with the wasp out of the adjacent unscreened toilet window.

Back in the bathroom, there was a bee dying in the sink. It had been a hot day, I thought, but I couldn't see where it and the wasp had gotten in. The bee's legs were moving slightly. I carefully let the tap run and the bee appeared to drink. It then crawled slowly around the sink.

When I returned this morning, the bee was curled over on its side. I laid it at the base of the screen next to the others.

This afternoon when I came home, our German neighbour and one of the neighbours who lives directly above us were on the landing talking about the pigeon. The neighbour who lives above us was holding a large pastel blue head of a hydrangea flower that she must have cut from our garden in one hand and two green reusable bags full of groceries in the other.

Our German neighbour said to me that she had been saying that she doesn't know how she did it, and please don't ask her how she did, but she'd taken the box with the dead pigeon that was full of maggots and swarming with flies to the bins. She said there had been three eggs in there. The neighbour from above put her shopping bags and the flower down on the storage box outside her apartment and started to sweep her landing. We never use that entrance, she said.

My German neighbour said she was sure it was the woman who lives above her who had left the box out and who had later removed the cardboard covering. She said there was shit everywhere. There was shit all through the box this high, she said, holding her thumb and forefinger apart to show the depth of the shit. You have to talk to her, the neighbour from above said. That's so horrible, I said, I'm sorry. Don't say sorry, our German neighbour said, it wasn't you.

Today a customer in the store said that the real estate market in a large city to the north of here has stopped altogether because of the continuous smoke. It's so dry here this year, she said, that it's undoubtedly our turn next. In a month or so, that'll be us, she said.

Handing me a children's book, the customer then said, could you please put this on hold until tomorrow. She turned to her daughter of seven or eight and said, please tell the man why we're putting this book on hold. I don't want to talk about it, the girl said quietly.

A few weeks ago, I mentioned to our German neighbour that I hadn't seen any dead bees on the driveway since I'd asked the gardeners to stop spraying. I don't doubt it kills insects, she said. She once worked, she said, for a large German chemical company.

Today, however, there were a number of dead and dying bees around the apartment building. On the car park asphalt near our garage door, a bee was slowly spinning around with wing buzzing and a great many ants around it. There were several dead bees down the side of the building, below Kelly's bathroom window, where they used to drink from a pipe that had been leaking but that has recently been repaired.

Earlier today when I phoned the twentieth-century modern furniture store to tell them about the crack through the base of the sofa, the person who answered asked if we'd sat on it. Such a shame my partner had said of the sofa, skimming her hand over the beautiful 1960s black and cream striped wool upholstery. I don't care if it's too big in this space, she'd continued, I can picture myself lying here all day.

I don't want to talk about it and I'm not dressed our German neighbour said to me when I went out to water the plants this morning. She was standing on the landing above me, pulling her robe tightly around herself. But the woman who lives above her, she went on, had yelled at her about removing the box. The neighbour had said to her, over and over again, that she must leave nature alone. It's not our place, she'd said, to interfere.

On the weekend, my partner and I walked a coastal trail to the south. We started the walk at a rugged beach that undulated along its length. The lower pits, darkened with black pebbles, would fill with each wave. The sea was murky and you could feel the weight and the power of the waves breaking only metres from the sand. In the distance, two surfers were catching the shortened waves, bailing almost as soon as they were on their feet. One of them paddled in and walked in our direction. He was wearing a black wetsuit and a white helmet. He was older, in his sixties. I nodded when he neared. He didn't respond but veered down an undulation into the shallow water.

At the end of the beach, the trail followed the rise of a low hill. The undulations, we could see from here, were almost perfectly even. On either side of us now, there were low eucalypts and wattles with black withered trunks. To see the beauty of this, my partner said, I have to imagine I'm from somewhere else.

Acknowledgments

An enormous thank you to Jessica Au, Ruby Todd and Antonia Pont for your generous and crucial readings and commentary, as well as to Shane Strange of Recent Work Press for supporting and trusting in this work. Thank you also to Maria Takolander for your supervision and astute reading of earlier pieces.

And, finally, thank you Pip, darling little rain water—it was an honour, and a deep kindness.

An earlier version of one of these triptychs appeared in *Rabbit Poetry*.

About the Author

Oliver Driscoll's debut poetry collection, *I don't know how that happened* (Recent Work Press), was released in 2020. Oliver co-runs the *Slow Canoe* live journal and chapbook press. He lives in Melbourne.

Printed in Australia
AUHW021014311221
357657AU00010B/23